The Mysterious Melody

Avril Rodrigues

BookLeaf Publishing

India | USA | UK

Made with ❤ on the BookLeaf Publishing Platform
www.bookleafpub.in
www.bookleafpub.com

Dedication

To my readers, whose hearts resonate with the quiet
whispers of the soul,
and to my family, friends, and acquaintances—
each of you has played a part in shaping my journey.
Your presence, support, and wisdom have been the notes
that
guided the melody of my life,
and through your encouragement, I found the courage
to listen to and share the unheard songs within.
This book is as much yours as it is mine.

Preface

There are moments in life when words become more than ink on a page—they become mirrors, reflecting the depths of who we are and who we are becoming. This collection is born from such moments. It is not merely poetry; it is a journey into the unseen, the unspoken, the truths that linger between heartbeats.

In a world that moves too fast, these verses invite you to pause. To reflect. To listen to the quiet voice within that often goes unheard. These poems are woven with depth, shaped by contemplation, and infused with the essence of transformation. They do not seek answers but rather awaken questions—the kind that stir the soul and shift perspectives.

Each piece in this collection carries its own weight, much like the lessons' life unfolds before us. Some will comfort you; others may challenge you, but all are meant to resonate in their own way. If you have ever found yourself standing at the edge of self-discovery, wondering what lies beyond, then these words are for you.

May this book be a companion on your path—a space

where you find echoes of your own reflections, strength in vulnerability, and the quiet power of inner knowing.

Welcome to the journey.

Acknowledgements

This book is the culmination of many voices, hands, and hearts that have shaped its path. To my friends, family, and Book leaf publication—thank you for your unwavering support, your guidance. You've provided the inspiration, love, and strength to carry me through every verse.

To those who have shared their stories, struggles, and moments of joy with me, your truths have become the rhythms and harmonies woven throughout these pages.

This book is as much about you as it is about me.

And to my readers—thank you for opening your hearts to the unheard melodies, for embracing the quiet truths that live within us all. You are the reason, for whom I have bared my soul.

With deep gratitude,

Avril Rodrigues

1. Life

I set out on an adventure,
Found myself on a roller coaster,
Titillating thrills, shivers down my spine.
But low and behold soon found myself
walking deep down towards a chasm,
A dirty, stagnant, lifeless pit.
Green moss, boat marooned & upturned
I stood aghast. No, not this.
Providentially saw another path,
out of this mess, out of this rut.
Discerned life's mystery
Fluctuating, in flux. Kaleidoscopic hues

2. Restless to Serene

Restless heart,
Uneasy spirit,
Stiff belly—
Where from, why now?
All was well.
The blame game begins,
Raging madness,
Clenched teeth,
Silent screams,
Everything topsy-turvy.
No, not me. Not fair.
What now?
Helpless tears.
Silence.
Deep sighs.
Cars honk, jars bonk,
Cooker whistles,
Pigeons twizzle,
Children's laughter,
Parrots chatter—

Oh, parrots, green, preen, serene,
Swinging, clinging, singing,
So free, so glee—
Heart soars,
Spirit glows,
World spins,
I grin.

3. The Winner

With a twinkle in his eye and a tingle in spirit,
A song in his heart and a swing in his step,
He dances through life, vanquishing all,
No challenge too great, no barrier too tall.

With grace and might, he conquers the fight,
A master of craft, both bold and bright.
Harnessing wind, earth, water, and light,
He wields their power with fearless insight.

And so, can we, if we dare to believe,
The strength lies within - just wait and see.
With hearts unshaken and spirits free,
We rise to embrace all we can be.

4. The Heart Speaks

Do this, do that.
Go this way, no that.
Contradiction a solemn predicament
Become an engineer you must.
Nay a doctor is far more justifiable
Climb the corporate ladder or be an entrepreneur.
To surf the countless voices,
pause, you must
and listen to the wordless voice of the heart.
It speaks the truth
Remaining alert, watchful, transcending duality.
Bringing clarity.
To escape confusion
center yourself and go within
Own your truth,
Live as truth- alive, radiant and blissful.

5. The Enlightened Rebel

I met a man—a rebellious man,
So daring and dauntless was he.
With fire in his eyes and a fearless stand,
He walked, defiant and free.
He strode against tides at the risk of his life,
Carving his path, leaving his mark.
Unafraid of what lay ahead. Not bound by the rules that
hollow men made,
He forged on through tempest and trial,
None could make him kneel.
He spoke not of war, nor battle, nor blood,
But with whispers of truth and armour of wisdom,
He shattered chains, unmasked fears,
And set men free.
A rebel of light was he!

6. Uncertainty

In the maze of dreams, where paths unfold,
He stood at the crossroads, timid yet bold.
His questions hung heavy, the world seemed unfair,
No answers in sight—just silence and air.

His heartbeat quickened, a fear unknown,
He searched for echoes of a throne.
The road stretched wide, yet shrouded in haze,
His future a whisper, lost in the maze.

He reached for hope, but it slipped like sand,
A wanderer bound by no guiding hand.
"Who am I to be? Where do I go?"
Chasing the answers, yet lost in the flow.

Through endless seeking, a truth took hold—
Growth lies in questions, in stories untold.
Through joys and sorrows, through shadow and light,
He found not an end, but the strength to ignite.

7. The Endless Call

In twilight's glow, where magic stirs,
His heart burned bright with painted swirls.
It whispered wishes, soft yet keen,
He chased the stars—he dared to dream.

With every step, his spirit soared,
He brushed his world in hues adored.
His soul took flight to endless skies,
Where visions danced, both bold and wise.

With mother's love and father's might,
He gave his all, he won his fight.
Through tireless days, through sleepless nights,
He carved his name in golden light.

Yet in his chest, a whisper grew—
A call that tugged, unknown to few
He looked around—what's this? What's missed?
His heart still called, so endlessly.

8. The Miraculous Change

There was a time when my hands clenched into fists—
knuckles whitening with the urge to strike;
my jaw tightened at the mere sight of him—
teeth grinding in suppressed fury;
my stomach knotted whenever I sensed a threat—
a visceral twist of apprehension.

I was impatient with life,
with myself, with the way the world moved -
too slow, too uncertain,
never bending to my will.
I rushed here and there,
ever seeking, ever questing,
my will, my way -
immediate but to where?

But with the passage of time, the echoes of who I was
softened.
Not all at once—

but in the quiet hours when no one watched,
in the hush of night wrapped around me,
when I let myself feel,
without shame, without judgment, without regret.

I learned that life was not in the chasing,
but in the slowing down,
in the breath between words,
in the silence of my heart,
steady as an evening tide.

Now my impatience has become presence,
my anger has melted into understanding.
And the echo of who I used to be
now walks beside me—
not as a shadow,
but as a quiet warmth of a lesson well learnt,
a gift of how it was truly meant to be.

9. The Tower

A flash of lightning cracks the sky,
exploding stones, topple down,
The tower falls, its glory lost
a steeple of pride now sadly ruined.

Flames consume the golden past,
walls once safe crumble at last.
Lightning speaks a dreaded truth,
shattering the fortress of youth.

From the ruin, a stirring roused,
through the bedlam, light arises,
freeing dreams that once were shackled
fear cannot withhold what's meant to be.

Let the tower fall, let it crumble down,
in its destruction --- divine intervention.

10. A Bolt out of the Blue

She was just eight, as pure as a seraph,
With chubby cheeks and curls so fair,
Her family's pet was she.

One sunny day, while at school she played,
Skipping stones, sneakers squeaking,
Amidst a symphony of glee,
Her father came to take her away.

Puzzled glances, silent sighs—
She knew not why
Her father came to take her away.
A dread she sensed,
As silently, nearer home came they.

A solemn crowd, hushed whispers,
Everything seemed grim and grey.
With wobbly feet, butterflies in her tummy,
Heart thudding, she spun away.

There on the bed, her precious grandma
Quietly lay.
She did not stir, no warmth in her hands,
Her face so pale.
No tender hug, no sparkling eyes,
No merry tales—
Though near, she seemed so far away.

Baffled by this uncommon sight,
She turned to her mother for instant clarification.
With a tear in her eye and a gentle sigh,
Her mother clasped her in a hug so tight.

Her mother's arms, warm and tight,
Yet no words could set things right.
She peeked again—was Grandma asleep?
Would she wake if she called her name?

The room blurred, the whispers swayed,
She held her breath and turned away.
Not knowing how, not knowing why,
She felt the weight of love lost that day.

11. The Dilemma

A child of six, a bundle of tricks,
Longing for love, for warmth, for touch.
Yet in her eyes, no love he found—
Only distance, cold and rough.

For daughters, smiles, a tender embrace,
For him—demands, an endless chase.
A mother's love—so harsh, unfair,
He wondered why it wasn't there.

He bore the weight, he played his part,
Gave all he had—his mind, his heart.
For sisters' dreams, he paved the way,
Yet love from her stayed far away.

She scorned his love, denied his hand,
Turned from where he chose to stand.
His joy, his wife—she cast aside,
Leaving wounds too deep to hide.

And now she lays with fleeting breath,
Calling for him before her death.
The wounds still fresh, the past still raw,
Should he go? Should he not?

To see her now—what would it change?
Could love be found in words estranged?
Or should he stay, let silence show
The weight of all she'd failed to know?

His thoughts weave through the years now gone,
Her absence long forgiven—did regret stir within?
Her repentance—a balm to his soul,
The key to end this agony.
Will he forgive, or turn away?
The choice is his—none else can say.

12. Whispers of Absence

She woke to a world drained of hue,
Morning so grey, no light drifted through.
The air lay heavy, no solace beside.
Her sorrow unyielding, locked inside.

Her heart echoed pain—unheard, unseen,
Lost in a fog where hope had once been.
She reached out—but no hand was there,
Only shadows whispering despair.

Memories blurred, once sharp and bright,
Her soul ached on, with no rest in sight.
She wore a mask, a practiced smile,
Drowned in her sorrow all the while.

The world moved fast; hers stood still,
A hollow shell, a broken will.
She longed for his touch, soft and sincere,
But all was dust—he had disappeared.

The mirror held a stranger's eyes,
Once filled with dreams, now blurred by cries.
The world moved on, so fast, so bright,
Yet she still waited through the night.

The weight of sorrow, sharp yet numb,
A battle fought, yet never won.
She reached for him, through time and space,
Longing just to see his face.

Then in the dark, she heard his voice,
as soft as dawn, as tender as dew ----
Not all is lost, though we're apart,
Our love lives on, forever in our hearts.

13. Redemption

She stood there, trembling,
terror sealed her breath,
the crowd stormed around, voices like shattered glass,
with stones in hand, ready to condemn her.
she had nowhere to run, none to defend her.

The first stone struck ---- a sharp, shearing, sting.
Then another and another,
her feet folded beneath her,
the dust swallowed her fall
her voiceless tears drowned, in the clamour around her.

Along came a stranger, so formidable and sure.
A hush fell as he knelt beside her,
she felt the warmth and strength of his hands as he
raised her,
he was no ordinary stranger, but her saviour.

He bravely held up his hand, and wrote in the sand,
"Let the one without sin cast the first stone".
A pause, a shift,
with uneasy glances, and shuffling feet,
One by one, the rocks fell; they drifted into the mist—
no one remained to condemn her.

So gentle his voice, her spirit so calm,
So boldly yet softly he quieted the storm.
He forgave her, he freed her, never cast her aside;
With pride in her gaze and a strong, steady stride,
She walked away—unburdened, unashamed, and free."

14. My Forgotten Friend

I found her on a lonely trail.
Nothing stirred, the air was still
bare trees, lined the mountain slopes
Shivering and alone
sunken eyes, pale cheeks,
My heart skipped a beat.
With a deep compassionate embrace,
I bid her leave the place.
swathed in a woollen cloak
mounted on my Pearly steed,
we cantered far far away
Bathed in warm sunshine,
with crispy wind against our skins.
our hearts soaring with the smells of Spring
Dancing among the daisies bright
Chasing bunnies left and right
picking juicy strawberries wild,
gently we lay on the meadow mild
soaking in the uplifting, soothing lavender swirls
She was me and I was she

We were one.
We were free.

15. An Exquisite Surprise

Woke up this morning graciously,
The sun shone down so brightly.
Birds sang their tunes audaciously,
I leaped from bed excitedly.

The scent of coffee filled the air,
Lifting my spirit sensuously.
I dove into my work speedily,
Fulfilling tasks rapidly.

Then rang the bell—so suddenly,
My friend stood there unexpectedly.
I embraced her tight, so full of cheer,
We danced and laughed happily.

We talked, we shared, with hearts so free,
A bond refreshed effortlessly.
Joy cascaded endlessly,
A gift of pure serendipity.

16. Creativity

Music is euphoric a whisper to weary hearts,
Painting takes you out of this world.
Poetry make sense of this unfathomable world.
Sculpture gives form to emotions untold.
Art strives to capture the soul.

.

An accomplished artist is a creator indeed.
Crafting with passion, visions and creed.
Yet none can match the hand that shapes each seed,
The ultimate source from whom all proceed.
Whose touch is glorious, boundless and free.

When the world feels heavy and makes no sense at all,
You too my friend, can break free,
from conformity.
connect with creative wisdom
to make everything upside down seem fine
Art is the life raft supreme.

17. Devotion

I don't know how I lived before,
drifting through days without a shore.
Since I met him, life is a dream,
burning bright with love supreme.

Without him, I am an empty shell,
his touch—a tide that makes me swell.
His presence sets my soul aglow,
a fire that only he can stoke.

He reads the silence in my eyes,
a whisper felt, a thought divined.
With every breath, he puts me first,
his love unbound; his heart immersed.

His tender gaze—an open book,
where love spills over every look.
Blessed am I to call him mine,
a love so rare, so pure, divine.

This must not end—my fervent prayer,
I'd chase his shadow anywhere.
In his arms, I taste the stars,
no need for more—this love is ours forever more.

18. You are Enough

You don't have to run,
you don't have to chase.
What you seek is already in you—
has been, and will ever be.

You don't need fixing,
you are not broken.
You are a river,
ever ebbing, ever flowing,
ever growing.

Breathe.
Stand still.
Feel the earth hold you.
You are enough—
as you are,
as you have always been.

19. Surrender

No more grasping at the wind,
no more shaping rivers' flow.
I kneel before the quiet tide,
unclenched, undone, unbound

The weight I bore was never mine,
the battles fought—an echoed dream.
I lay it down in silent conviction,
knowing love's tender touch redeems.

No walls remain, no guarded gate,
no need to chase, no need to prove,
silent, still, serene --- I move,
surrendered into something new.

20. Veins of the Infinite

I feel her in the hush between my breaths,
a quiet thread that pulls me home.
Not here, not there—just always,
a spark burning bright, woven through the fabric of life.

She hums beneath my fragile skin,
a knowing pulse unseen, yet felt
as gentle as the wind that stirs,
the fragrant blooms upon the hill.

No edges mark where I begin,
no line divides what I can be.
The infinite is not beyond—
she lives, she moves, she's me.

21. The Silent Witness

In the hush between heartbeats,
in the stillness beyond time
a whisper stirs the silence—
a voice - I wonder whose?

It speaks not of the future
nor the echoes of the past,
but something vast, unspoken,
in the present holding fast

It asks for neither striving
nor a path to be made clear,
only presence in the stillness,
only bids you hear.

Beneath the endless wanting,
beyond the self's disguise,
rests the watcher of the moment,
ever watchful ever wise

No need to seek it's meaning,
no need to chase the light—
just rest within the moment,
a feeling of pure delight.

22. The Infinite Spark

Beyond the name we are given, beyond the face we wear,
something ancient stirs within, neither bound nor bare.
Beyond the roles we identify with, beyond the tether of
time,
a voice hums in the core sublime.

It speaks in the hush between twilight and dawn,
where silence sits shimmering still and shorn
It lingers in the echoes of the past now long gone
its essence, enhances exchanges --- the old into the new.

It is not the breath, yet the wind knows its name,
not the fire, yet it dances in the flames.
It is not the water yet it flows endlessly,
a ripple unbroken in an infinite stream.
It is the dreamer, the dream, and the dreamed.

www.ingramcontent.com/pod-product-compliance
Lightning Source LLC
La Vergne TN
LVHW010931200726
843509LV00013B/2167